Eva Hoffman   and   Yvonne Handford

C000064844

MIND MAPPING IN PRIMARY CLASSROOMS

LEARN TO LEARN

Copyright © 2004 Eva Hoffman & Yvonne Handford

All rights reserved.

The moral rights of the authors have been asserted
in accordance with the Copyright, Designs and Patents Act 1988.

No part of this book may be reproduced, stored or transmitted in
any form or by any means, electronic, mechanical, photocopying,
recording or otherwise, without prior written permission from the
publisher.

The publisher grants an exception to the purchaser of a master
copy of this book to make copies of the activity pages for their
own classroom use only.

ISBN - 0 9535387 96

Published by LEARN TO LEARN

LTL Books Ltd.
17 Westlands Road
Middlewich
Cheshire
CW10 9HN - UK
Tel +44 (0)1606 832 895
Fax +44 (0)1606 837 645
www.ltlbooks.co.uk
info@ltlbooks.co.uk

Printed in England

'Mind Maps®' is a registered trade mark of
the Buzan Organisation, Poole, Dorset, UK.

'PlayStation®2', 'PlayStation' and 'PS2' are registered trade marks
of the Sony Computer Entertainment, Inc.

MIND MAPPING IN PRIMARY CLASSROOMS

PRACTICAL HINTS, SUGGESTIONS AND SOLUTIONS FOR TEACHERS AND PARENTS

Contents

Contents

INTRODUCTION

In the late 1960s and early 1970s Tony Buzan* experienced a profound insight into the way people learn, which resulted in the creation of a brilliant and most versatile learning tool, he called mind mapping.
Since then he, Vanda North and many others have been spreading the word and teaching millions of people around the world how to use it.

Tony Buzan differentiates between
> **note-making** (coming up with ideas which originate in your head)
and **note-taking** (putting on paper ideas coming from an outside source such as a book, a lesson or a TV program).

Mind mapping is primarily based on two concepts: **associations** and **key words**.

How often do you find yourself listening to someone talking about something and before you know it you are thinking about something else you have just been reminded of? This thought takes you to another thought, and soon you may be thinking about something seemingly unconnected with the original idea.
Mind mapping reflects the way the brain works by using a radiant format combined with associations. As a chain of associations goes on and on, it facilitates creativity and can lead to fascinating new ideas or even great discoveries.

I (Eva) am frequently asked whether making spider diagrams is the same as mind mapping. It is not the same.

> Mind mapping
>> reflects the way the brain works by using radiant format combined with associations,
>> draws on the whole, left and right brain (words, pictures and colours),
>> automatically provokes organization of thought and
>> is a great memory tool due to the use of associations, key words, clear printing, images and colour.

> Spider diagrams
>> give information connected with the topic in the centre only,
>> draw primarily on the left brain (words),
>> do not influence the way material is organized and
>> do not aid memory in the same 'wholesome' way.

* Mind Maps® is a registered trade mark of the Buzan Organisation, Poole, Dorset, UK.

Who is mind mapping for?

In our experience mind mapping suits about 95% learners, particularly those who
    have a need to see the Big Picture before they get down to details,
    naturally focus on details and need help in grasping the Big Picture,
    don't easily express their thoughts in writing,
    write a lot but find organization of their thoughts tricky,
    find colours and pictures helpful in memorizing information,
    get stuck when attempting to come up with new ideas,
    struggle with concentration,
    feel overwhelmed with the sheer amount of information they need to absorb,
    want to spend less time studying and make it much more enjoyable.

Who may not want to use mind mapping?

We have come across some learners who
    find curly lines messy,
    do not want/need/like to use colour,
    do not respond to or even notice the existence of pictures,
    find black letters on white paper very satisfactory,
    do not feel the need to change the way they learn.

If those learners have given mind mapping a chance and still don't like it, we have to accept that it is not for them.

The experience we have had using mind mapping with children as their learning tool has been truly amazing.

I (Yvonne) once asked a number of children, some of them with various Special Educational Needs, what they liked best in school. I expected them to tell me that it was art, games, or computers, things most children would normally list as their preferences. To my amazement, the almost unanimous response was: 'MIND MAPPING'!
I introduced a Year 4 S.E.N. boy to mind mapping a few months ago. Previous to that he had very low self-esteem,

he showed scant interest in lessons, had difficulties listening to explanations and instructions, and produced very little written work. His response to mind mapping was fantastic! He realised that he could actually make great 'map notes' and that he could understand them! The knock-on effect was almost immediate; his self-confidence rocketed, his concentration improved, he became keen to join in discussions and was able to complete work to a good standard for the first time in his life.

It is interesting that when using mind mapping, the gap between children with different levels of ability seems to decrease dramatically. The standard of work of some children with S.E.N. is in fact very similar or even, in some cases, better than mainstream. S.E.N. children who begin by mirror-writing their words on the left side of the mind map soon learn how to do it correctly.

In schools where I (Eva) have worked, using mind mapping has considerably improved children's attainment, thinking, creativity, and clearly added variety and fun to learning – not something to be sniffed at!

In our experience mind mapping really suits boys, many of whom dislike writing and tend to produce the bare minimum in the way of work; mind mapping turns those boys around in a flash.

It wouldn't be an exaggeration to say that it has been a saving grace for many young people; discovering and acquiring this new skill has lead many to frequently unexpected successes. Mind mapping gives children confidence and they quickly start producing their best pieces of work yet.

A Year 6 teacher, whose class was involved in transition work to Year 7, had many pupils who were finding the language activities very challenging. However, some excellent work emerged once their class teacher had encouraged them to use mind mapping to plan their work.

Finally, thanks to mind mapping, children are finding Key Stage 2 revision work infinitely easier!

Although mind mapping is undoubtedly becoming more widely used in schools, there are still many which fail to introduce children to this uniquely helpful learning (and teaching) tool. We still meet educators who haven't come across it or don't fully recognise its benefits.

In my work with teachers I (Eva) have encountered teachers who know about mind mapping but have not yet grasped its versatility and tend to limit its use to one or two applications.

These teachers frequently ask about other ways they can use the tool and want to see examples of its applications.

This book is our response to those requests. This collection of activities focuses on examples of how you can use mind mapping in your classroom or with your child individually.

Pages marked with are ready-made activity sheets which can be photocopied and given to your children. Teacher/Parent pages contain examples and brief explanations of numbered activities.

In order to make things clear and simple, most examples in this book have only three or four main branches, but it is important to remember that mind maps® may have many more branches, as many branches as many topics we wish or need to explore. It is not uncommon for a revision map to have ten or more branches.

If you need more information about the skill or wish to better understand the theory behind it, see our list of recommended books.

We hope that this collection of exercises will encourage those teachers and parents who are vaguely familiar with the tool but have not yet developed enough confidence to use it with their children, as well as those who need to be introduced to a wide variety of examples before they can start making full use of it when teaching children.

We also hope that by introducing mind mapping to many more young learners, this book will be our contribution to making their learning more effective and much more enjoyable.

Eva Hoffman   and   Yvonne Handford

PRINCIPLES OF MIND MAPPING

The coloured picture on the next page illustrates the basic mind mapping principles.
These principles need to be remembered and used consistently, and so they become automatic
by the time children start mind mapping on their own.

Draw a central picture representing your subject/topic using three or four colours.

Branches start at '1 o'clock' and go clockwise around the picture; draw each branch in a different colour.

It is important that branches underline words and that you print words rather than use longhand, and that you draw as many pictures as possible.

Connected branches emphasise the connection (association) between words, while **printing** will have a big impact on memorising information when mind mapping becomes a memory/revision tool.
Pictures/symbols help us memorise things, while colours not only help our memory by adding clarity to the 'picture map', but make it more fun, too.

It is important to remember that while we normally *write* words from left to right, we *read* an association chain sequence always from the central picture outwards: – topic, subtopic, details, etc.

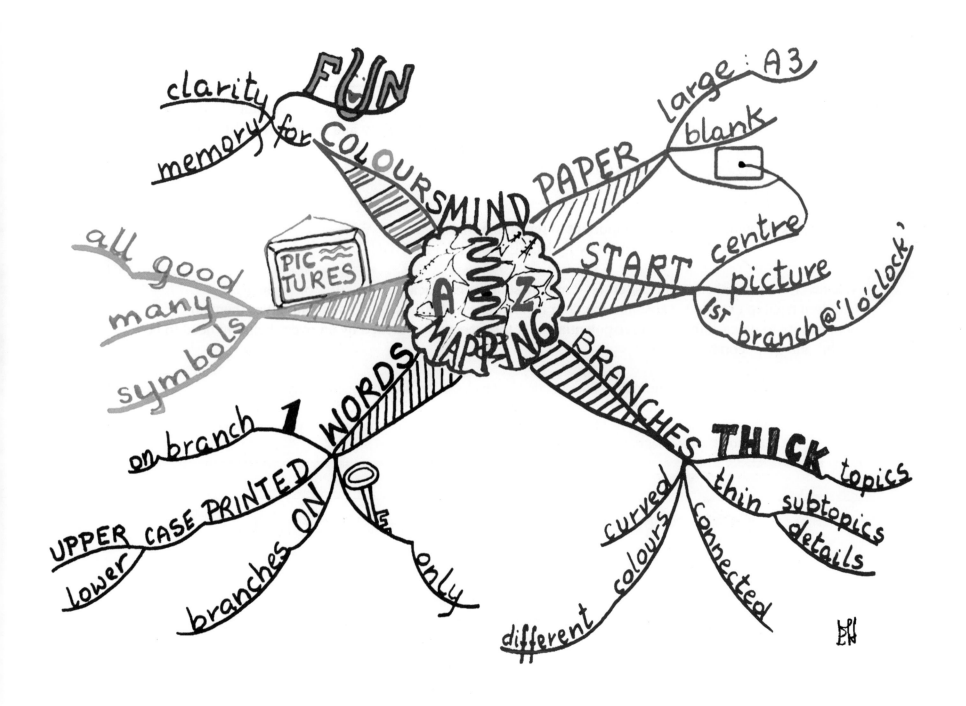

ASSOCIATIONS

Before we immerse ourselves and the children in the mind mapping activities, it is important to make sure that everybody understands the concept of associations; that **association flow** and **association bloom** are understood and well practiced through group games and activities.

Start by practising association flows (also referred to as **association chains**) as a group game without any handouts.

When working with children it is important to remember that
> EVERY ASSOCIATION IN NOTE-MAKING IS RIGHT.

Whatever comes to their minds is 'correct' and must never be discarded as 'silly' or 'wrong'.
Children need to experience absolute freedom in making associations. Mind mapping gives them an opportunity to unleash their creative potential, only too frequently blocked by an overwhelming need to be 'right' and give 'correct' answers.

Warning: Our school curriculum does not devote much time to promoting creativity.
Bearing in mind how preoccupied we all are with making sure children **absorb** information, we needn't be surprised that it may take some time before the children you teach feel truly free to let their imaginations run wild again.

hedgehog → needles → thread

ice → icecream → cone

<u>Example</u>

Look at the picture on the left...
On line 1 write or draw a picture of the thing that comes to your mind when you look at it.
On line 2 draw or write what comes to you when you think about the word (or picture) on line 1.
On line 3 write or draw what comes to you in connection with the picture or word on line 2.

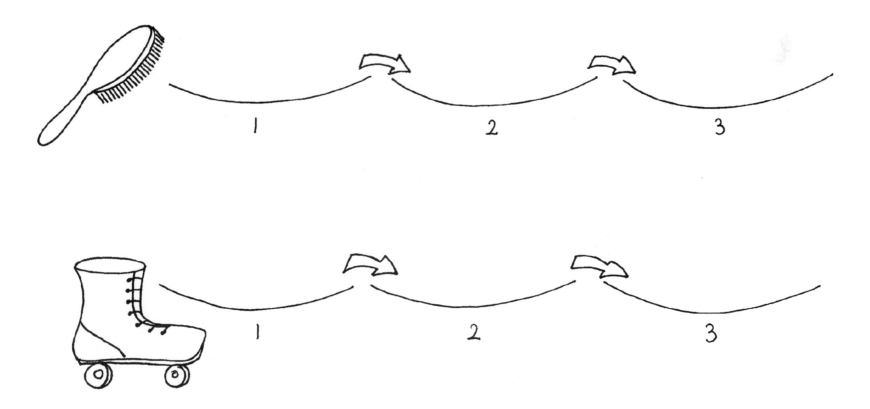

1   2   3

1   2   3

Compare your lines with someone else's and see how different your associations are.
Isn't it amazing?

ASSOCIATIONS

This activity takes the concept of associations further, leading to **association bloom**.

Below is one example of how this 'milk bottle' activity could be developed,
showing one expanded 'branch family' (the thick branch with its thinner branches).

Example

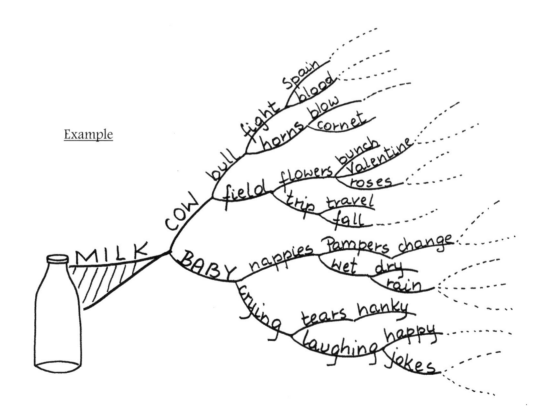

On the very thick branch coming out of the picture, write or draw what comes to your mind when you look at or think about a bottle.
On the branches coming out of the thick branch write or draw two things that come to you when you think about the word or picture on the very thick branch.
Now on the thin branches write things that come to your mind when you think about the word/picture on the previous, slightly thicker branch.

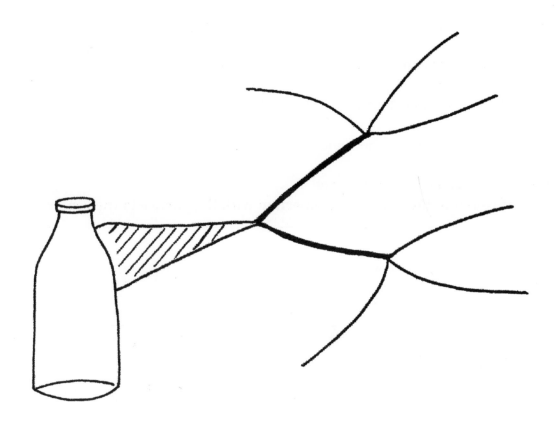

Remember that everything that comes to your mind is right. You simply cannot go wrong here!
When writing, PRINT your WORDS on branches and make sure branches underline your words.

2

ASSOCIATIONS
(TOPIC - SUBTOPIC)

Let children choose their own topics or choose one for the whole class.

Ask children to positioned their blank pages horizontally (landscape).
 Then ask them to draw a picture of their topic in the 'cloud' in the middle
 of the page, using three different colours.

The first key branch appears at '1 o'clock', as indicated here.

Ask them to colour the branch and draw (or write) on it
 the first thing that comes to their mind in connection with the picture in the centre.

Helping children plan their maps on a page.

 Our experience shows that many young children are not sure how to find the middle of the page.
 To help them, you may suggest that before they start, they draw or imagine two diagonal lines
 crossing in the very centre of the page.
 Also, some children draw very tiny, hardly visible pictures representing their topics, while others
 cover the whole page leaving hardly any space for the branches. Practice will help them get the balance right.

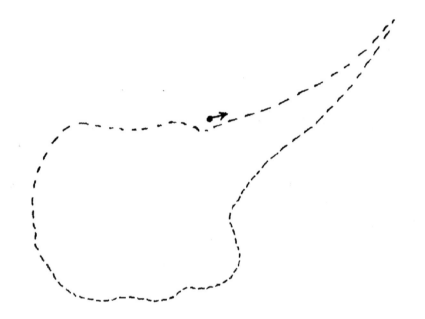

ASSOCIATIONS
(TOPIC - SUBTOPICS)

- Children colour in the thick '1 o'clock' branch and then draw or write on it the **first thing** that comes to them when they think about shoes (topic).
- Then they take another colour, colour in the second branch (at '5 o'clock') and write or draw **another thing** that comes to them when they think about shoes.
- They do the same thing with the remaining two branches, using a different colour for every thick branch.
- Then they draw thinner branches and print or draw on them something connected with the words/pictures on the thick branches (subtopics).
- Encourage children to compare their maps to see how different the associations can be.

You can use one of the blank 'star maps' for any other subject/topic.

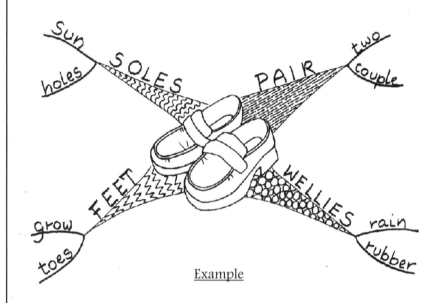

Example

The blank 'Star Maps' provided on the following pages can be used in a variety of ways.

Young children, children lacking in confidence, or children with Special Educational Needs will benefit from this 'dotted map' approach; they can confidently go over the branches with their colouring pens.

These dotted base maps can be used to develop further associations with the same topic in the centre. They can also be used to practise association bloom with different topics in a 'proper' mind mapping format, and as base maps for more advanced exercises.

Arrows on the branches indicate where to start writing (some children tend to write backwards, unless instructed otherwise).

Note that all branches are curved so that they are as horizontal as possible. This way the paper stays in one position. It also helps when they learn to read their maps and makes remembering them considerably easier.

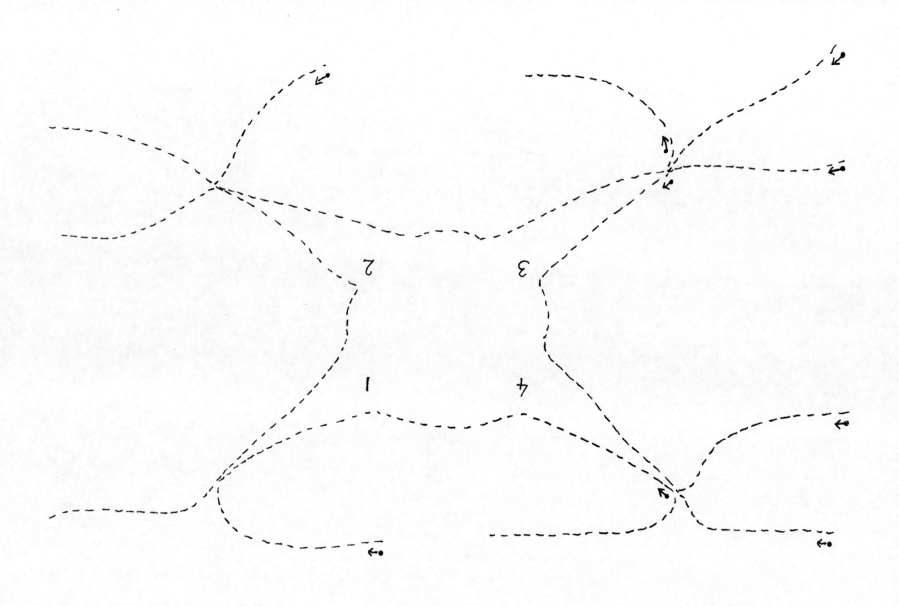

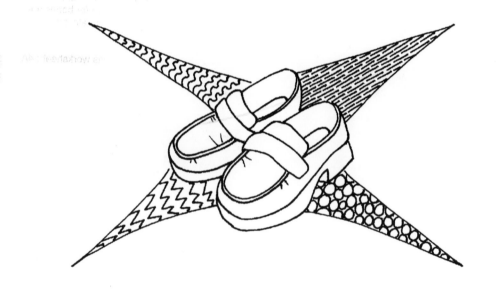

4

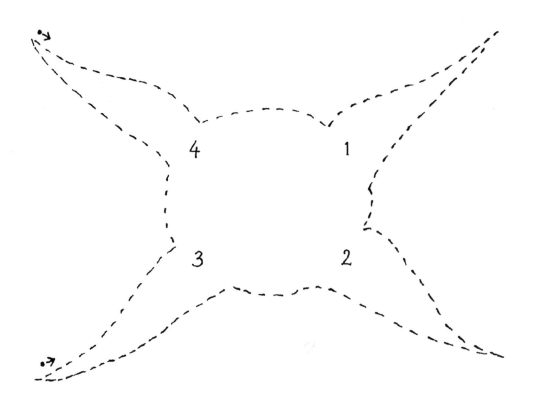

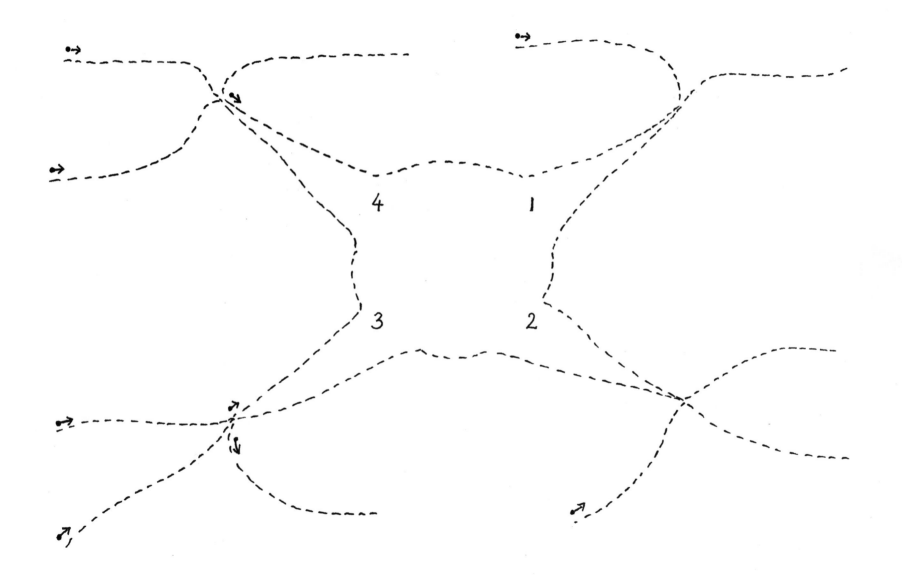

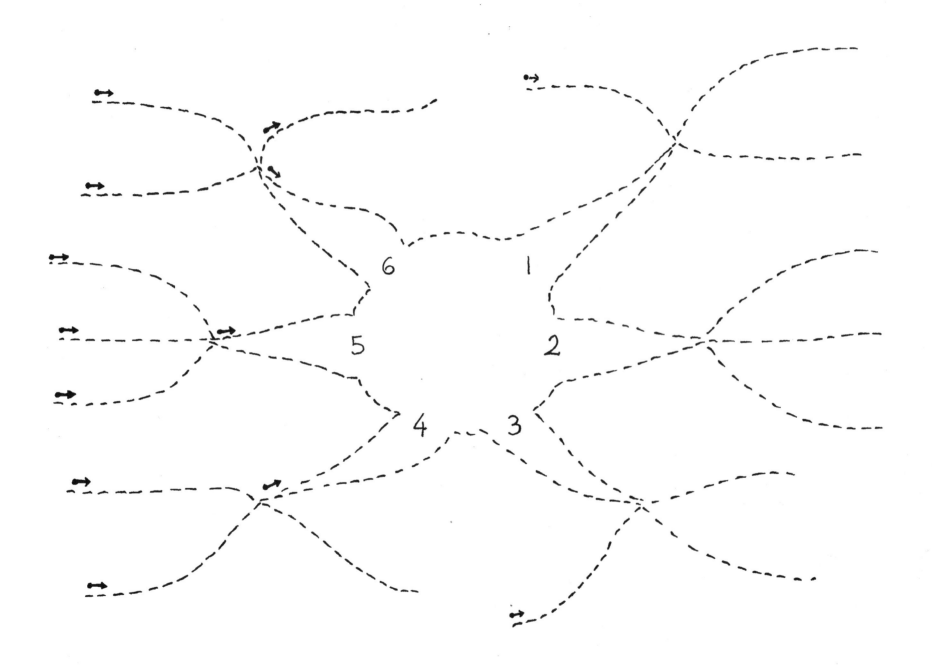

ASSOCIATIONS

The aim of this activity is for children to practise *recognising associated words* and *putting them into sentences*.

If you think it necessary, photocopy the Star Map on A3 size sheets to make sticking pictures on branches easier.

Ask children to colour each branch a different colour.
Find pictures corresponding with each season and circle them in the same colour as the branch.
    (Example:
        if they colour the SPRING branch green, the *daffodil*, the *lamb* and the *tree with leaf buds* will be circled green).

Tell children to begin with the SPRING branch.

When all the pictures have been cut out and glued to the sheets, ask children to put the words from the branches into sentences.
    (Example:
        In spring daffodils grow in the garden.)
        In autumn leaves fall off the trees.

Colour the picture using a different colour for each 'branch family'.

Take the same colour pen with which you have coloured Spring and circle all pictures which remind you of Spring. Do the same with the pictures which remind you of the other seasons.
Cut out the pictures and glue them to the branches where they belong.

5

ELEMENTARY SPELLING AND READING OF CVC WORDS
(Consonant – Vowel – Consonant)

Ask children to colour the branches using a different colour for each branch family.
Have them underline/circle/colour the corresponding words and pictures on the placer strips to match the colours of the letters on the thick branches.

Start with the **- a -** branch.

Example:

if the letter **- a -** branch is red, underline **pan   rat   tap** with a red marker.

When the maps are ready the words can be read out in chorus.

Help children make 3D prism 'placers' as shown below;
encourage children to use the blank placer grid to make their own placers.

① 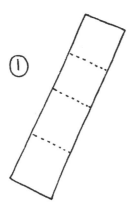 ② 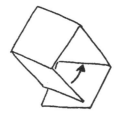 ③

Put the placers on the corresponding branches.
Use some glue or tiny bits of Blu-Tack to hold them in position.

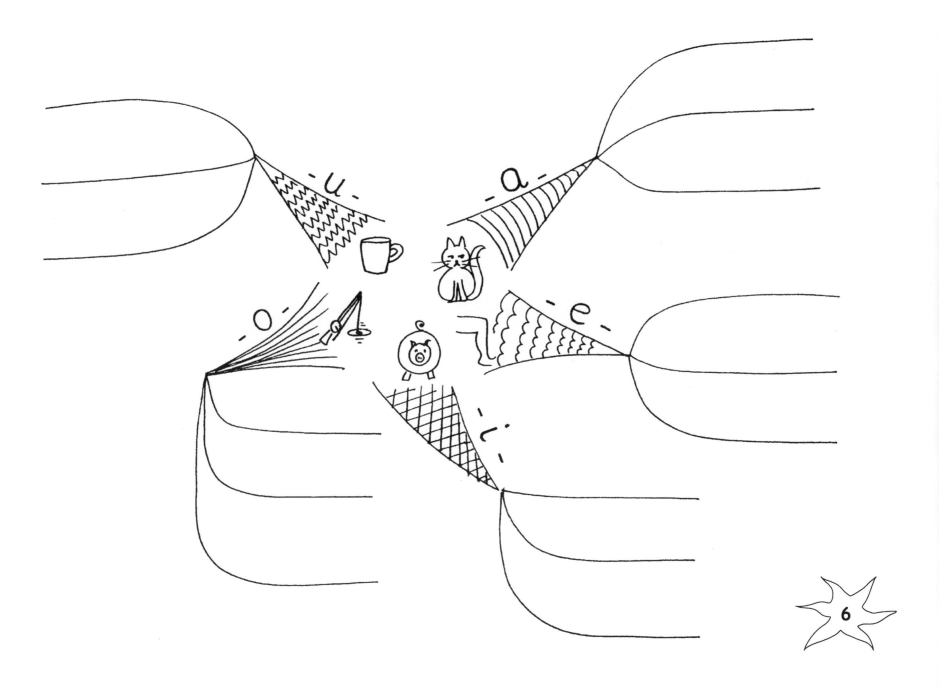

6

YOUR OWN PLACERS

Cut out and make a little tent from each placer strip, folding them as shown.

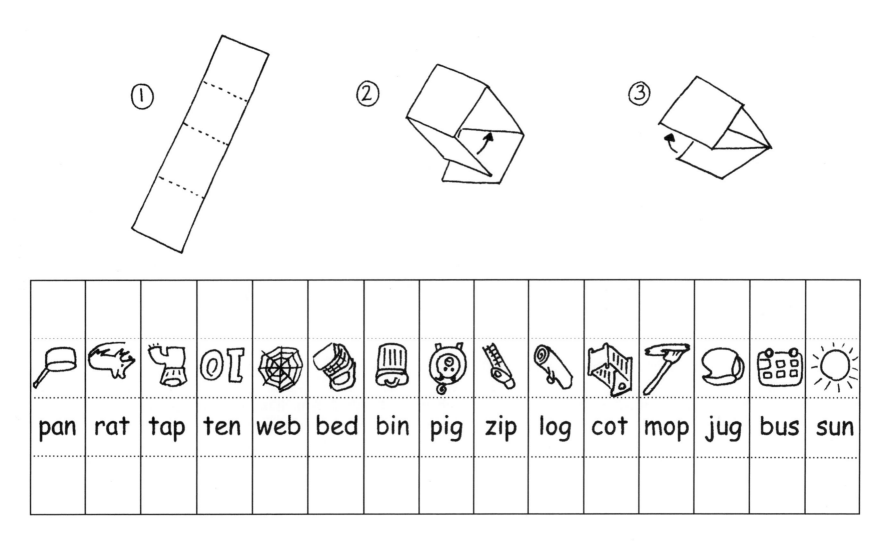

① ② ③

| pan | rat | tap | ten | web | bed | bin | pig | zip | log | cot | mop | jug | bus | sun |

6

PRACTISING READING LONGER WORDS
(WORDS WITHIN WORDS)

Spotting words within words is not only a fun game, it also helps children read longer words with more confidence and become more sensitive to the way they are spelled.

If possible, photocopy the maps on A3 sheets to make fitting the words on branches easier.

Children colour in the five long words, each with a different colour, then on the '**words**' map they colour each branch family with one of the same colours.

Next they find the short words that are parts of the longer ones, and colour them with the same colour as the longer ones within which they appear
      (Example: '*screwdriver*' will be the same colour as '*screw*', '*drive*' and '*crew*').

Children cut out the longer words and stick each one on the thick branch of the same colour.

Then they cut out all the remaining words and stick them on the matching thin branches.

Colour in all the longer words in the first column on the left. Use a different colour for each word.
Now, using the same set of colours, colour the branches of the 'words' map using a different colour for each 'branch family'.
Now look at the shorter words. Can you spot any of them in the longer ones?
Colour them in the same colour as the longer ones they appear in.
Cut out the longer words and put them on the corresponding thick branches.
Cut out the shorter words and put them on the same colour thin branches connected to 'their' longer word.

screwdriver	screw	command	vest
investigate	return	gate	cover
discovery	and	drive	discover
commandment	disc	able	crew
returnable	invest	turn	men

When you have glued all the words to their branches, first read one set of short words and then read the long word. Is it easier to read it now?
Do the same with all the other words.

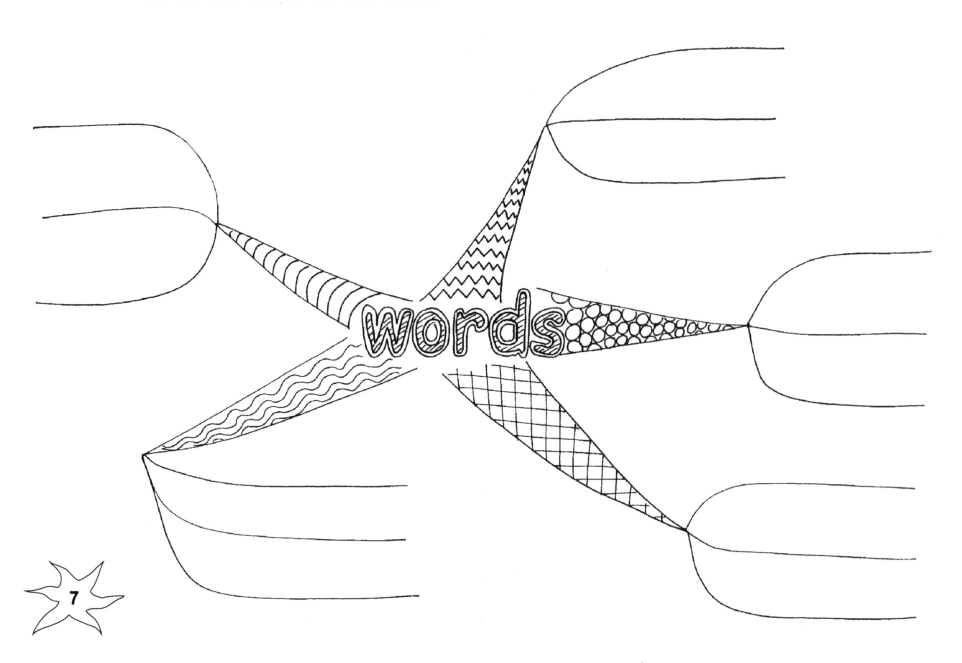

7

PLANNING A STORY

Fables are a great way to introduce children to planning a story using radiant notes; a fable is usually short, straightforward, with a definite beginning, middle and end.
The moral of a fable, 'it teaches us', appears on the final branch.

First let children **listen** to the fable and follow the story on the dotted picture map **while listening**.
If you see they are getting lost, indicate which branch they need to be looking at.

Then you may want to give children copies of the fable and encourage them to read it and find
the information **they are reading about** on their maps.
Enlarge the text of the fable if you are working with children who struggle with reading.

Children colour in the maps using a different colour for each branch family.

Once you have read the fable and the maps have been coloured, ask children to tell the story to each other, branch after branch, using all the words and pictures on the maps as a visual aid.

As mentioned earlier, young children, children lacking in confidence, or S.E.N. children will benefit from this 'dotted' mind mapping approach to a story plan; they can go over the branches with their colouring pens.
They can also use it as a model for mind mapping other fables or stories.
For more elaborate stories you can use or prepare dotted 'star maps' similar to the ones provided earlier (Activity 4).

The Lion and The Mouse

One day, a lion caught a mouse by its tail.

The kind lion took pity on the mouse and let it go free.

The mouse said that he would never forget the lion's kindness.

Some time later the lion got caught in a trap set by hunters.

The lion roared trying to struggle free from the net.

The mouse heard the lion's roar and ran to help.

The mouse nibbled a hole in the net and the lion was able to escape before the hunters returned.

This fable teaches us that if you are kind to others,
they will be kind to you.

8

Listen to the fable 'The Lion and the Mouse'.
Go over the dotted branches and words using a different colour for each 'branch family'
(the thick branch with its thin branches, words and pictures).

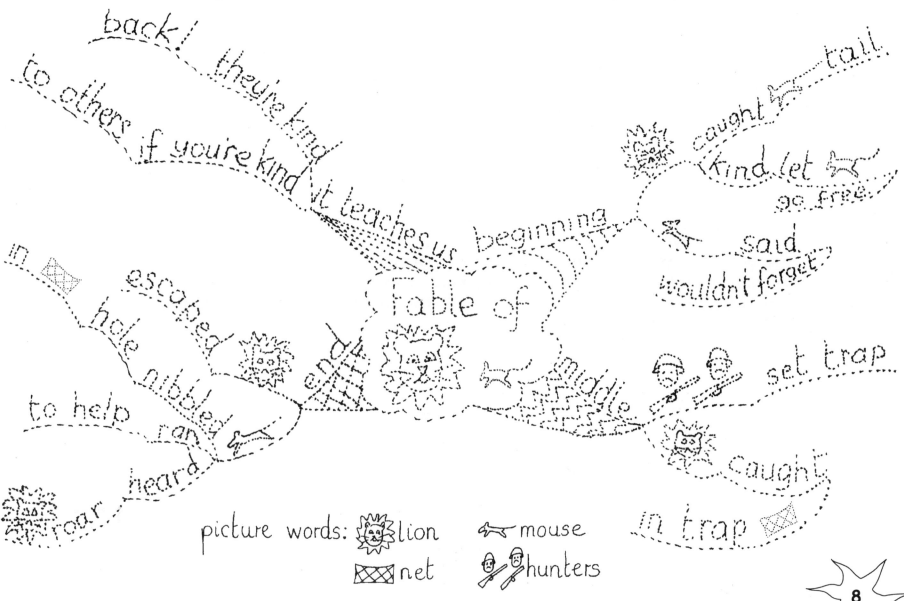

picture words: lion   mouse
net   hunters

Tell someone the story using your visual map to help you remember the details of the story.

MIND MAPPING A STORY PLAN

This activity encourages children to start **taking** radiant **notes** without the pressure of finding the key words. Here, the map has all the necessary branches, thick and thin, and the words are given to them to be put on the map frame, where appropriate. At this stage, despite emphasising earlier the mind mapping rules, children may put a few words on each branch. Identifying key words will come later.

The Fox and The Crow

One day a fox was feeling hungry.
He noticed a crow above him in a tree holding a piece of cheese in her beak.
The crafty fox told the crow that she had a lovely voice and asked her to sing to him.
As soon as the crow opened her beak to sing, the cheese dropped down to the ground.
Quickly, the hungry fox gobbled up the cheese.
The crow flew off, very annoyed.

*This fable teaches us that it is not good to be vain
and that we can't always believe what others say.*

- Read the fable to the children and ask them to write on the thick branches:

  Beginning   ***Middle***   ***End***   and   ***It teaches Us***

- Then ask them to write the associated words and phrases on the thin branches.

- When all the writing is completed, children can tell the story to each other.

Listen to the fable and put the words and phrases from the table on the corresponding branches.
Draw pictures wherever you want. The arrows show where you need to start writing words or phrases.
Use 4 colours, one for every 'branch family' (the thick branch with its thin branches, words and pictures).

BEGINNING	MIDDLE	END	IT TEACHES US
fox hungry	fox asked crow to sing	fox gobbled cheese	it's not good to be vain
crow in tree	crow opened beak	crow flew off	we can't always believe everything
cheese in beak	cheese dropped	crow annoyed	

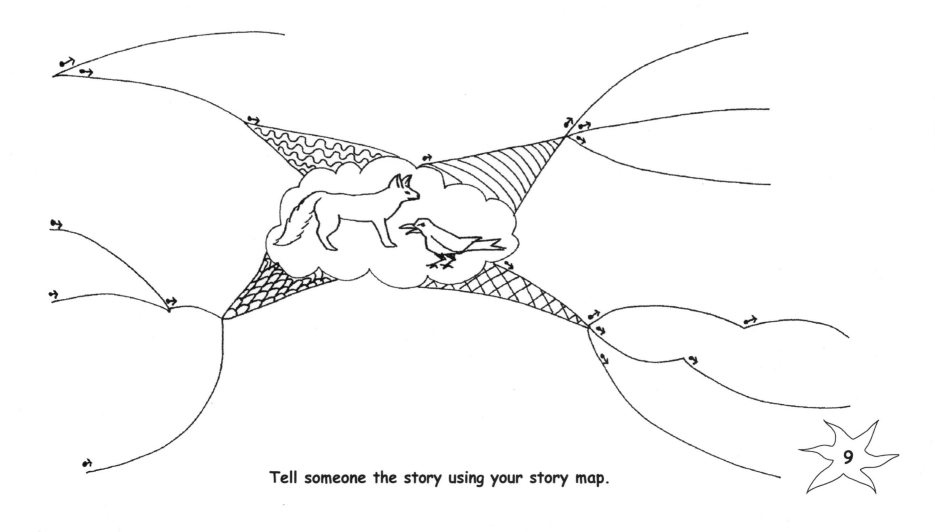

9

Tell someone the story using your story map.

TAKING NOTES FROM THE TEXT

To make it easier, in this activity the key words on the thick branches are already given.

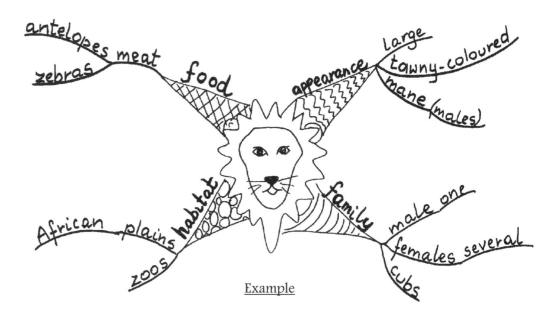

Example

You can do this work with children in two ways.

1. Tell children to
- **read** the text themselves
- colour in the branches of the map
- **read the text again** and highlight the associated words in the text in the same colour as the appropriate branch
    (Example: if the words '*appearance*' and its branch are blue, then words like '*large*' and '*tawny-coloured*' will be highlighted in blue)
- **draw** the necessary number of **thin branches** and transfer highlighted words onto the corresponding branches, one branch at a time.

2. With a more advanced group, ask children to colour the branches and, **while reading the text, highlight the appropriate words and put them straight away on the corresponding branches**, adding thin branches as necessary.

Lions

Lions are large, tawny-coloured wild cats.

Adult males weight about 180 kg. Females (lionesses) are slightly smaller and have no mane. Lions usually live in groups called prides. A pride has one male, several females and their cubs. Lions often hunt as a team. No other big cats seem to do this. They are meat-eaters, eating mainly antelopes and zebras. Lionesses do most of the hunting.

As well as living on the plains of Africa, many lions today lead protected lives in zoos and on nature reserves where they are safe from human hunters.

Read the information about lions.
Colour in branches and highlight appropriate words in the text in the same colours
as the branches they relate to.
Add thin branches and write on them the highlighted words.

Looking at your map, tell someone what you have learned about lions.

TAKING NOTES WHILE LISTENING

This activity is useful for children with a strong preference for kinaesthetic learning,
as well as for children who find writing challenging.
It is ideal for working in pairs.

Photocopy the 'Cyclops' map on A3 size paper, if possible.

Tell children to
- **listen** to the Greek myth 'Odysseus and the Cyclops'
- colour in the words '*beginning*', '*middle*' and '*end*' in three different colours and use the same colours for the placers in each section
- put the three main words on the three main branches of the mind map and colour them in the same colours
- cut out and put the placers in the right order on the corresponding thin branches
  (if you are not planning to use this activity again, ask children to glue their placers to the branches)
- **tell** someone the story
- **write** the story USING their mind maps as their story plans.

Encourage them to make use of the words from the given word bank.

Odysseus and The Cyclops

Odysseus and his men were sailing home after a long voyage.
They were very thirsty and very hungry. By now they had very little water to drink and very little food left. Suddenly they saw an island and decided to land there to look for food and water. As they got closer, they noticed that the island had steep cliffs with lots of caves. Once they were on the island, Odysseus and his men were amazed to find giant-sized goats, the biggest they had ever seen. They followed them into a cave.

Suddenly the ground began to shake and the most enormous man they had ever seen entered the cave. It was the Cyclops, Polyphemus. He had just one eye in the middle of his forehead. He stared angrily with his one eye at Odysseus and his men. All of a sudden he grabbed two of the men and ate them! Then he lay down at the entrance of the cave and fell asleep. Odysseus had an idea. He found a log and together with his men he sharpened it to a point , until it was like a huge spear. Quietly they climbed up the Cyclops' massive stomach and rammed the spear into his eye, the one eye on his forehead. The blinded Cyclops screamed in pain. Then he sat by the entrance of the cave to stop anyone from escaping.

Clever Odysseus told his men to get under the goats and cling to their bellies so that the Cyclops wouldn't know they were there. As the Cyclops let the goats out of the cave, he felt their backs but not their bellies and he didn't notice Odysseus or his men. They all managed to escape. They ran back to their ship and quickly set sail.
When Cyclops realised what had happened, he roared with anger. He climbed up the cliff and threw boulders towards the ship. However, as he was blind and couldn't see what he was doing, he missed.
The ship sailed safely home.

Listen to the Greek myth. Colour in the branches and the corresponding placers.

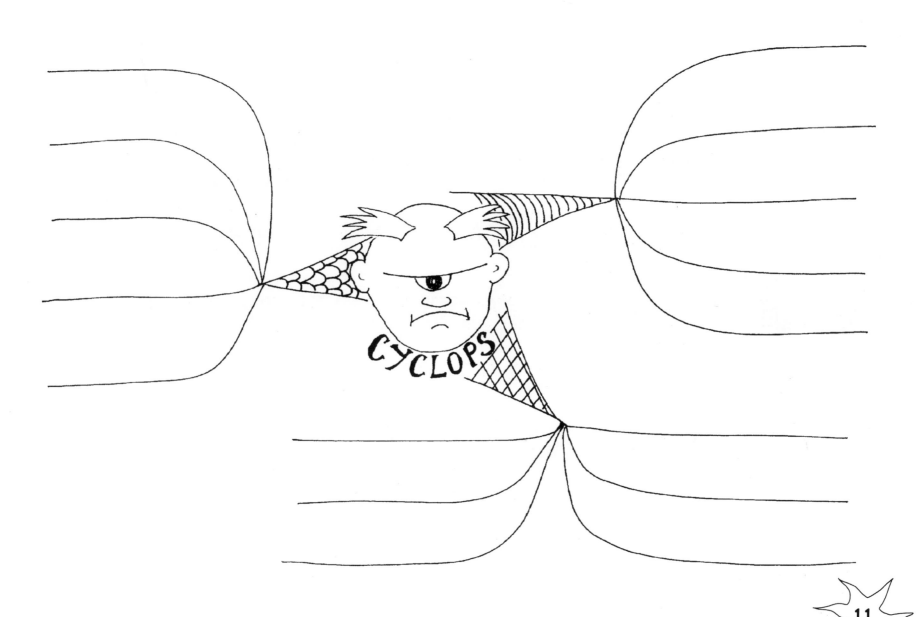

Put the placers on the thin branches and tell someone the story USING your story map.

THE CYCLOPS - Placers

beginning	middle	end
(sailor, three men, ship)	enormous, 1 (eye)	(sailor, three men) escaped
very little (bucket, food)	(cyclops fist) ate (two men)	clinging under (goats)
(ship, island with palm)	asleep	roared, climbed (tower)
giant-sized (goats)	(sailors, log)	threw (rocks)
(sailor, three men, cave)	rammed (eye)	(ship) sailed away
	blinded, screamed	

THE CYCLOPS - Word Bank

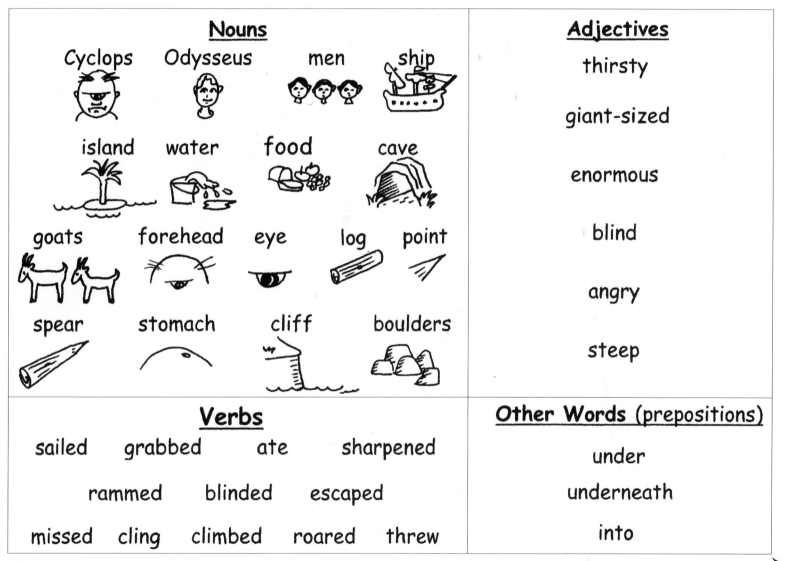

Nouns

Cyclops   Odysseus   men   ship

island   water   food   cave

goats   forehead   eye   log   point

spear   stomach   cliff   boulders

Adjectives

thirsty

giant-sized

enormous

blind

angry

steep

Verbs

sailed   grabbed   ate   sharpened

rammed   blinded   escaped

missed   cling   climbed   roared   threw

Other Words (prepositions)

under

underneath

into

11

The Cyclops

Write your own story. Each branch on your map can be a separate paragraph and the Word Bank can help you with the spelling. Draw your own picture of the Cyclops in the square next to the title.

Tell children to
- **listen** to you reading them the whole story
- colour in the branches and draw thin branches coming our of the thick ones
- listen to the first part of the story and write the associated words or phrases on thin branches
- now listen to the 'middle' part of the story and do the same
- and finally, listen to the 'end' of the story and do the same
- **tell** the story to someone
- **write** the story USING their maps as a story plan.

When doing this or similar exercises with a higher ability group, you may ask children to write information as soon as they hear it, trying to sort the *beginning*, *middle* and the *end* sections themselves.
Then ask them to **write the story**.

The Legend of Mu-lan

The Huns were invading China.
Mu-lan's father was told that he had to fight the Huns but he was too old. There was no grown-up son in the family so Mu-lan decided that she would join the army instead of her father.

Mu-lan bought a horse and went off to fight the Huns, pretending to be a man. Mu-lan was a very brave soldier. As a reward, she was asked if she would like to be promoted. Mu-lan replied that all she wanted was a horse so that she could return to her family as quickly as possible.

When she arrived home, she was welcomed by her family. She took off her soldier's clothes and returned to her old life as a girl.
Her friends in the army were amazed when they discovered that the brave Mu-lan was not a man at all!

Example

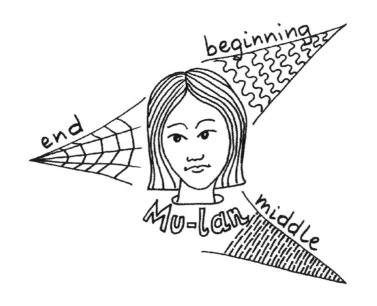

beginning

end

middle

Mu-lan

VERBS AND ADVERBS

Tell children to
- **read** the fable and colour in the thick branches using three different colours
- **find** and highlight corresponding **verbs** and put them on the branches
  (Example: if the hare branch is yellow,
  the verb '*bounced*' will be highlighted in yellow too)
- **think of adverbs** which **could go** with the verbs, and write them on added branches (they may think of some funny ones…)
- **tell** someone the story and then **write** it USING their own map as a plan.

Hare

bounced . happily
leaping
flying
hopped
skipped
stopped . suddenly
flopped
yawned

waved
loudly . shouted
hooted
clapped
madly . cheered

crowd

Hare·Tortoise
Verbs·Adverbs

Tortoise

followed . slowly
trudged
stumping
appeared
plodding
steadily . shuffled
passed

Example

Help children with additional questions such as:
How did Hare bounce/hop ? (quick**ly**, light**ly**, enthusiastical**ly**, energetical**ly**)
How did the crowds shout ? (loud**ly**, mad**ly**, happi**ly**)
How did the tortoise move ? (heavi**ly**, thoughtful**ly**, patient**ly**, steadi**ly**)
Alternatively you may make a list of adverbs and ask children to match verbs with adverbs.

The Hare and The Tortoise

'Ready, steady, go!'

The crowd waved and shouted. What a race it was going to be!

Hare was away first. He bounced forward as fast as he could go,
leaping and almost flying through the air.

Tortoise followed, trailing behind him.

He trudged down the road, stumping along. How could he win?!

Hare bounced, hopped and skipped until he was out of breath.

He stopped and flopped down to have a rest in the shade of a tree.

He yawned, his eyes closed and he fell asleep.

Then Tortoise appeared, plodding along.

He passed Hare who was still snoozing, and shuffled on.

Hare yawned, rubbed his eyes and gasped as he saw Tortoise
beat him to the winning line.

The crowd hooted, clapped and cheered.

People were so surprised to see Tortoise win!

13

crowd

Hare · Tortoise

Verbs · Adverbs

Hare

Tortoise

13

READING A MIND MAP®
and practising WRITING DESCRIPTIVE PROSE

Children often make picture maps of stories and then ignore them completely when writing the actual text.

In this activity there is no text so children have to read the mind map® to be able to write a description of the room.

Help children put the words on the first two branches into sentences.

Then encourage them to work in pairs and put the remaining words into full sentences.

Remind them that the words on the thin branches describe or give more information about the words on the thick branches.

<u>Here is an example of what the text may look like.</u>

The Forgotten Room

Slowly, the door creaked open...
Inside the room the faded wallpaper was peeling off the walls. Through the grimy window the weak winter sun made a half-hearted attempt to penetrate the gloom.

The fireplace was a gaping black hole. Its tiles were broken and cracked. On the mantelpiece were old yellowing photographs of a family dressed in their Sunday best. There was a dull brass clock which made no sound, as if the time had stood still.
The carpets were threadbare, with dusty floorboards showing through. A sofa and chairs with ripped upholstery and broken legs were leaning sadly against each other.
As mice scuttled inquisitively from cracks in the skirting board, spiders were stringing their webs across each corner of the room.
Then slowly, the door creaked shut on the forgotten room.

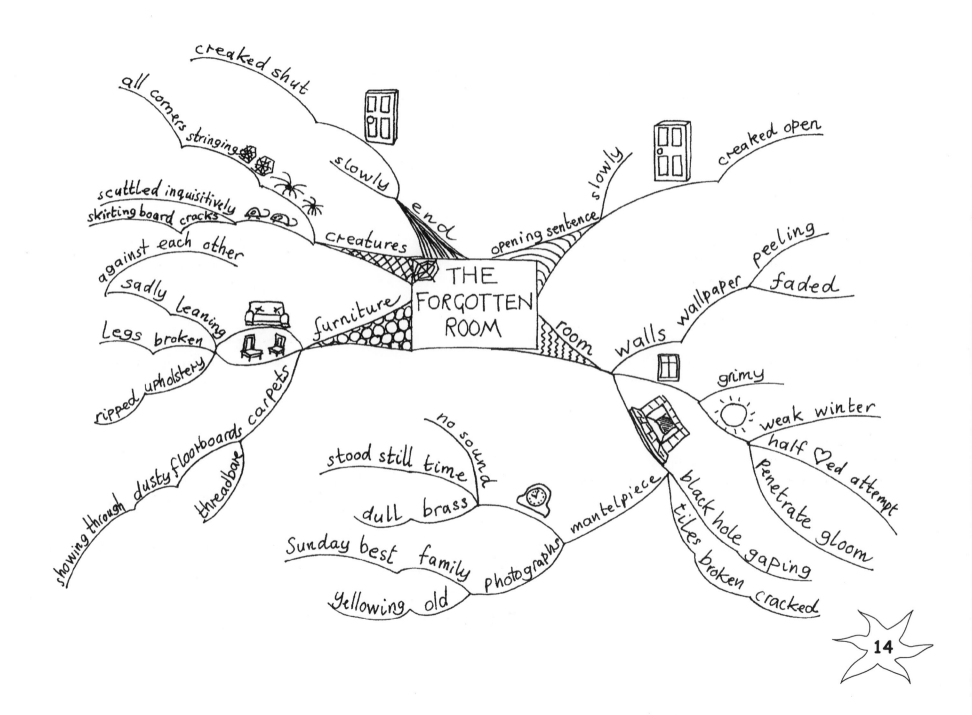

THE FORGOTTEN ROOM

creaked shut

all corners stringing

slowly

end

scuttled inquisitively

skirting board cracks

creatures

against each other

sadly leaning

furniture

Legs broken

ripped upholstery

showing through dusty floorboards carpets

threadbare

no sound

stood still time

dull brass

Sunday best family

Yellowing old

photographs

mantelpiece

opening sentence

slowly

creaked open

walls wallpaper peeling

faded

room

grimy

weak winter

half ♥ed attempt

penetrate gloom

black hole gaping

tiles broken cracked

14

PLANNING CHARACTER DESCRIPTIONS
AND WRITING THE PLANS IN A LINEAR FORM

Ask children to
- think of a character, who could be fictional or non-fictional, alive or dead, someone they know or they just have heard of
- 'dress' their character, drawing their face, hair, clothes and any accessories, if appropriate
- select from the list appropriate key words and PRINT them on the thick branches
- add thick branches, if necessary
- draw thin branches and PRINT on them any information they want.

It may be a good idea to remind the children about the rules.

- IN THE MIDDLE OF A LANDSCAPE PAGE DRAW A PICTURE REPRESENTING THE TOPIC
- BRANCHES START AT '1 O'CLOCK' AND GO CLOCKWISE AROUND THE PICTURE
- PRINT YOUR WORDS - WRITE ONE WORD ON EACH BRANCH - MAKE THE WORDS 'SIT' ON THE BRANCHES
- DRAW AS MANY PICTURES AS YOU CAN
- USE COLOURS - COLOUR EACH SET OF BRANCHES DIFFERENTLY

Think of a character you want to describe.
Select the key words appropriate for your character from the list and PRINT them on thick branches.
Draw as many thin branches as you want and PRINT on them your ideas.

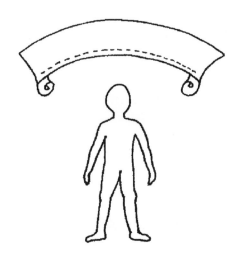

Occupation
Appearance
Personality
Likes
Dislikes
Family
Friends
Achievements
Dreams
other?

15

PRACTISING PLANNING AND WRITING A DESCRIPTION

Ask children to imagine a secret garden with all the plants, animals and old things that could be there.
Tell them it is their garden, and they can make it how they want it to be.

Ask them to think
- **what** could be in the garden
- **what** these things could be **like** (adjectives)
    (Example: *old, rusty, crumbling, broken*)
- **where** they could be
    (Example: 'an oak tree' – 'old' – 'in the corner near the wall').
Ask the children to make a mind map®; decide what to write on the main branches and add thin branches with
    descriptive information on them (encourage children to use two or three adjectives to describe every noun).

When they are ready, ask children to write a description of their secret gardens USING their mind maps®.

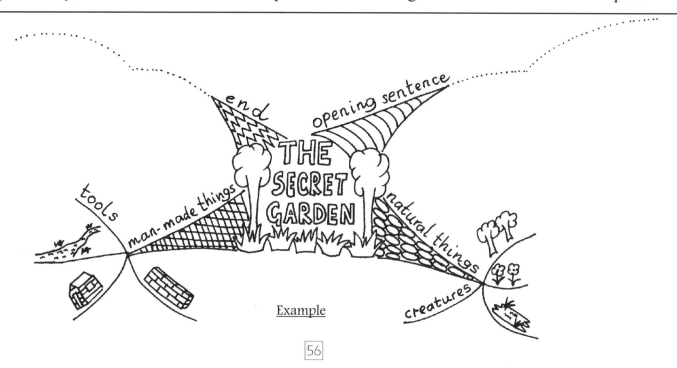

Example

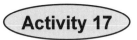

MIND MAPPING A POEM AND PLANNING A POEM
based on a mind mapping model

Ask the children to read the poem ('Desert Man' in this example).
Help them organise the information into relevant groups as shown in the example.

Ask the children to
- PRINT the key words on thick branches, COLOURING each branch in a different colour
- draw some thin branches and PRINT on them all appropriate information.

Example

The same 'star map' can be used as a base for another exercise.

Ask the children to
- think about, say, the life of homeless people living in the streets
- make a mind map® about, e.g., a 'Street Man'
- put down any ideas they may have (they may choose to write a happy poem!)
- write their own poems USING their mind maps® as plans.

Desert Man

On a sweltering, hot day
a man wanders
across the burning sand.
He seems lost and confused,
has no purpose or direction.
He takes off his jacket
as the fierce rays of the sun
beat down on him
relentlessly.
There is no shade to protect him.

His eyes squint into the distance
through the hazy heat.
His mouth is dry and parched,
beads of sweat cover his blistered skin.
He calls out for help but nobody hears him.
The man is alone.
Exhausted, he sits on the burning hot sand
dreaming of an ice-cold drink
and a soothing, long dip in an icy pool.
A lovely dream on this sweltering, hot day.

17

READING FOR INFORMATION and READING COMPREHENSION, as well as LISTENING COMPREHENSION and NOTE-TAKING

You can do this exercise in three ways.

READING FOR INFORMATION

- Ask children to first **look at** the Mary Rose map one branch after another to get an idea of what information they need to find,
- then ask them to **start reading** the text and write the missing information in the blank spaces on the map **immediately** as they come across it.
- Ask them to **tell someone the story** of the event and then write it out in full **using the completed mind map®**.

READING COMPREHENSION

- Ask children to **read the text first,**
- **then** to **look at** the Mary Rose map and fill in the blanks *as they read it again*.
- Ask them to **tell someone the story** of the event and then write it out in full **using the completed mind map®**.

LISTENING COMPREHENSION

- Tell children to **listen** to the story and while listening
  look at the mind map® one branch after another to get an idea what information they need to find,
  and as soon as they hear appropriate information to print it on branches.
- Ask them to **tell someone the story** of the event and then write it out in full **using the completed mind map®**.

With a more advanced group of children you could vary this activity by asking them to add branches and write on them as they listen to the story or read it themselves (Activity 18b).

The Mary Rose

The Mary Rose was built in 1509 in Portsmouth.
It was named after King Henry VIII's sister. The Mary Rose was the first purpose-built warship, designed to attack enemy ships from a distance.

An inventory for the Mary Rose dated 1512 stated that she was manned by 120 sailors, 251 soldiers, 20 gunners, 2 pilots, 5 trumpeters and 36 servants.

She was considered to be a very successful ship of the time. It came as a big shock when, in 1545, the Mary Rose keeled over and sank – in full view of King Henry VIII. It is believed that most of the 415 members of the crew and some 300 extra soldiers also died. This happened as the Mary Rose was being prepared to attack the French fleet.

The wreck of the Mary Rose was eventually raised in 1982, using large cranes and inflated airbags. Gradually thousands of items have been retrieved from the wreck and preserved. These items include guns, skulls, clothes and tools. They provide valuable information about life at sea during Tudor times.

No-one knows why the Mary Rose sank. One of the theories is that the crew were incompetent and failed to lock the portholes.

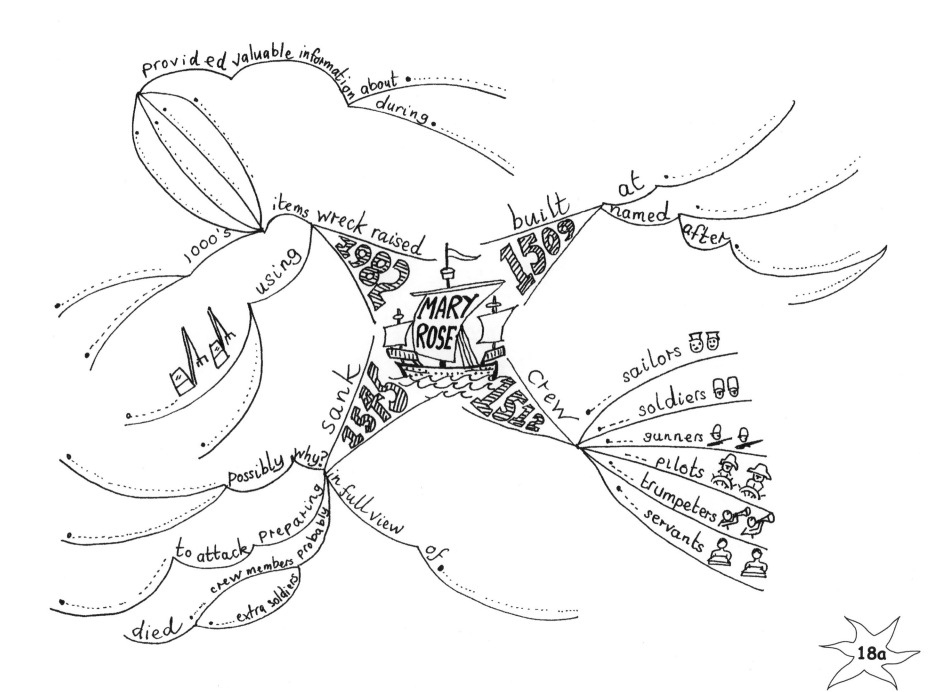

provided valuable information about ·········

during ·········

items wreck raised

built at ·········

1000's

named after ·········

using

1509

1982

MARY ROSE

sank

crew

1545

1512

sailors

soldiers

gunners

pilots

trumpeters

servants

possibly why?

Preparing in full view

to attack

of ·········

crew members probably

died

extra soldiers

18a

MARY ROSE

1982   1509

1545   1512

18b

LISTENING COMPREHENSION AND NOTE-TAKING

Tell children to
- **look briefly at** the incomplete Buddhist Monk map
- complete the map by filling the blank spaces while **listening to you reading the text**
- use the completed mind map® to **tell someone the story**
- use the completed mind map® to **write the text** in full.

Becoming a Buddhist Monk

In some countries, like Nepal and Tibet, Buddhist boys become monks for a few months of their lives. This helps them to reach enlightenment.

Their heads are shaved and they are allowed to wear monks' robes, which are usually red or orange.
Parents take the boys to a joining ceremony.

The parents treat their Buddhist monk sons with respect. Parents also gain merit when their sons become monks.

Buddhist girls may become nuns in a similar way to the boys becoming monks.

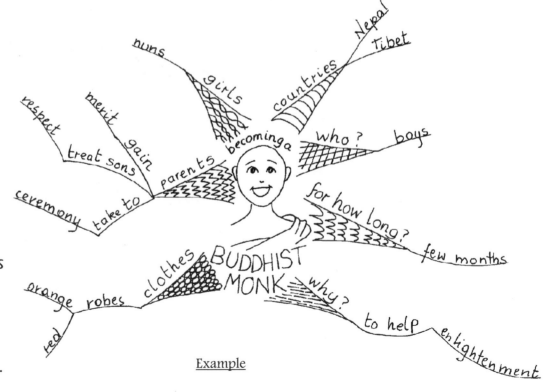

Example

Complete your radiant notes, then write what you know about Buddhist Monks using your map as a plan.

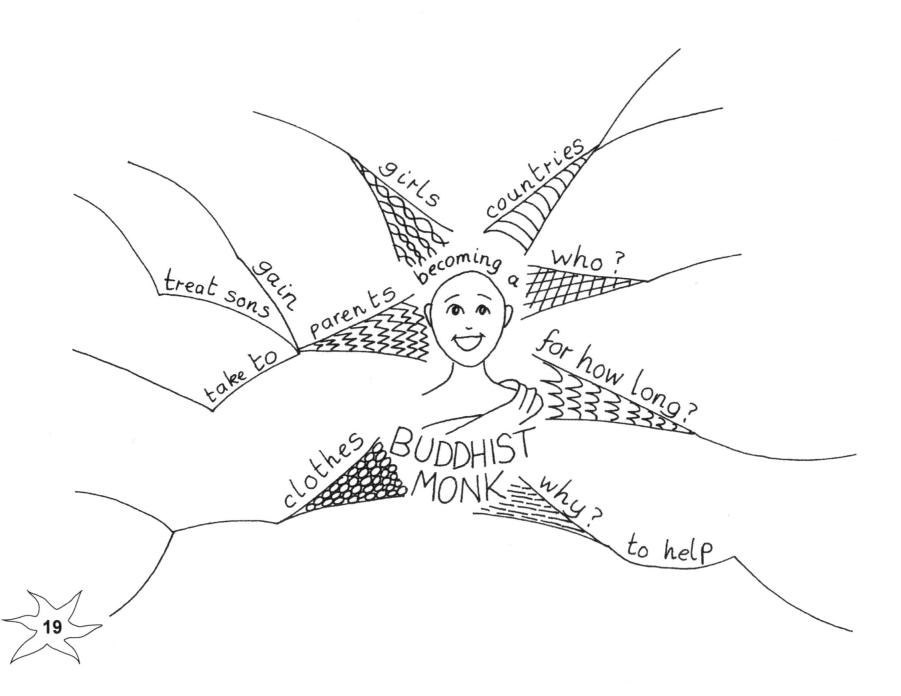

girls

countries

gain

becoming a

who ?

treat sons

parents

take to

for how long ?

clothes

BUDDHIST MONK

why ?

to help

PLANNING A COMPOSITION
on a given subject with no information provided

This activity helps children to organise their writing by teaching them paragraphing.
Information on each 'branch family' (the thick branch and its thinner branches) becomes one paragraph.

Tell children to
- think about or look at the picture of PS2 and on the '1 o'clock' branch write the first thing that comes to their mind in connection with it
- do the same thing with the remaining 4 branches, colouring each in a different colour
- draw thin branches coming out of the first branch and add information about the word on the thick branch
- do the same with the remaining branches
- tell someone your thoughts about the topic
- write a text (composition) about the topic remembering that the information on each branch family needs to be one separate paragraph.

Let children think of their own ideas.

If, after a while, you sense that they are running out of ideas
- suggest they exchange ideas with a partner
- prompt with your own thoughts or
- suggest subtopics as in the example shown on p.68.

Here is another way you may do this activity.

Frequently there are two or even three key words in a sentence. Children need to be able to decide which one is the KEY key word and which key words will follow on the next branches.

In the middle of the board draw a picture of a subject (PS2 in this example), then draw five branches and print on them main subtopics, e.g.: TOY, USERS, CHALLENGES, DANGERS, GAMES. Taking one branch at a time, ask children to think for a moment and let you have any thoughts that come to them in connection with words on the main branches. Write ALL the children's thoughts on the flipchart. Together with the children, find key words in their sentences and write them on the thinner branches coming out of the thick ones.

Children copy the map and illustrate words with pictures and symbols.

Below are a few examples of what YEAR 5 children have come up with when talking about PS2.

'PS2 is a *great* **toy**'.

'*Mostly* **boys** like it a lot, but *some* **girls** like to play it too. Many **adults**, more *men* than women, love it'.

'You need to be **quick**, you have to **concentrate** a lot. Completing higher **levels** can be very *difficult*'.

'You want to spend *a lot* of **time** playing the game. Sometimes you just have to **complete** a level'.

'Sometimes your **eyes** *hurt* when you play for a long time'.

'People want you to do other things (homework, meals) and this is very **irritating** for everybody'.

'There are *many* **games**'.

'Some games are for *younger* **children**, others are marked for **teens over 15**'.

'Games are very *expensive* unless you buy second-hand ones; they are called '*pre-owned*', then they are **cheaper**'.

'Some games are *funny,* but many are quite *violent*'.

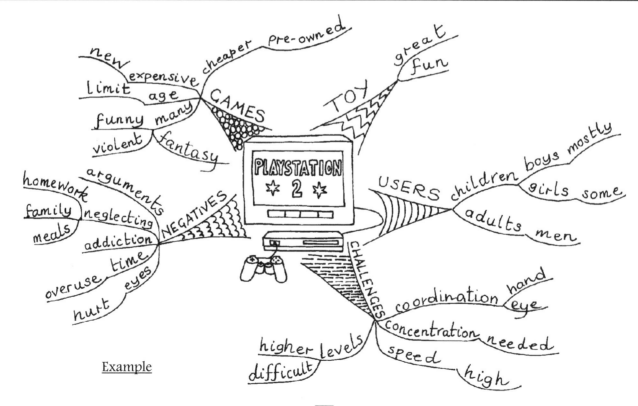

Example

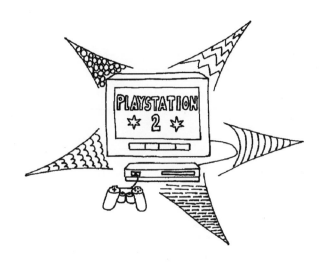

DEVELOPING CREATIVE THINKING WITH MIND MAPPING

Think of a controversial topic, or ask children to come up with a few and write one or all of them on the board.
Then ask children to draw a picture representing their topic and on the three branches coming out of it print:
- PLUSES, - MINUSES, and - INTERESTING.

Inspire children to come up with all the reasons why this, whatever it is,

•   is a GOOD idea

•   all the possible reasons why this is a BAD idea

•   and some reasons why this may be an INTERESTING idea (neither good nor bad)*

and put their reasons (using preferably only the key words) on as many thin branches as they need.

> * Edward de Bono called this type of lateral thinking exercise '**Plus – Minus – Interesting**' (see bibliography).

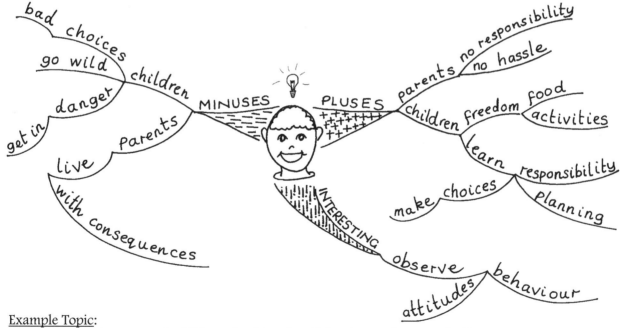

Example Topic:
        Once a week children should make all decisions at home and tell parents what to do.

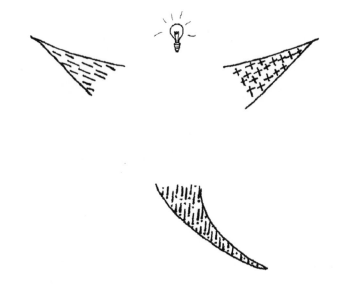

Tell somebody your arguments and listen to theirs. See if they are similar or different.

21

PROBLEM SOLVING WITH MIND MAPPING

Think of something that is a genuine problem for children in your school, something that really matters to them.

> Say: *This is a problem and we need to do something about it.*
> *What do YOU think should be done?*

Ask them to come up with ideas how this problem could be resolved. Encourage children to feel free to suggest any solutions even if they sound unreasonable.

At this stage every idea is acceptable and needs to be taken into consideration.

Write children's ideas on the board and help them find all key words which will appear on thick and thin branches.

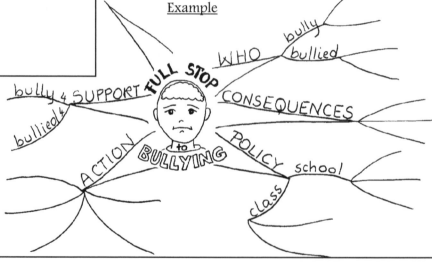

Example

Remind the children about the rules.

- IN THE MIDDLE OF A LANDSCAPE PAGE DRAW A PICTURE REPRESENTING THE TOPIC
- BRANCHES START AT '1 O'CLOCK' AND GO CLOCKWISE AROUND THE PICTURE
- PRINT YOUR WORDS - WRITE ONE WORD ON EACH BRANCH - MAKE THE WORDS 'SIT' ON THE BRANCHES
- DRAW AS MANY PICTURES AS YOU CAN
- USE COLOURS - COLOUR EACH SET OF BRANCHES DIFFERENTLY

Think about a problem you need to solve and draw a picture of it in the middle of your page.
Draw branches coming out of the picture and write all ideas that come to your mind.
Share your ideas with others, give them some of yours and add to your map some of theirs.

Now read your thoughts again and giving each a number put them in order
from the best to the least helpful (1 – the best).
Tell someone your thoughts, then write a composition following your plan.

PLANNING A BOOK REVIEW

Help children plan the first book review using this tool.
Once they have seen an example, they will be able to apply this structure to review any book of their choice.

Before they start, have them mindmap the story/the plot of the book; help children identify the key events
(see Activities 8, 9, 10, 11, 12, 13).
Ask them to draw additional branches connected with the ones in the picture and print on them all the information about the book.

When they complete their maps, ask them to
- put key words into sentences
- tell someone their thoughts about the book and
- write the book review using their mind maps® as plans.

It may be a good idea to remind the children about the rules.

- IN THE MIDDLE OF A LANDSCAPE PAGE DRAW A PICTURE REPRESENTING THE TOPIC
- BRANCHES START AT '1 O'CLOCK' AND GO CLOCKWISE AROUND THE PICTURE
- PRINT YOUR WORDS - WRITE ONE WORD ON EACH BRANCH - MAKE THE WORDS 'SIT' ON THE BRANCHES
- DRAW AS MANY PICTURES AS YOU CAN
- USE COLOURS - COLOUR EACH SET OF BRANCHES DIFFERENTLY

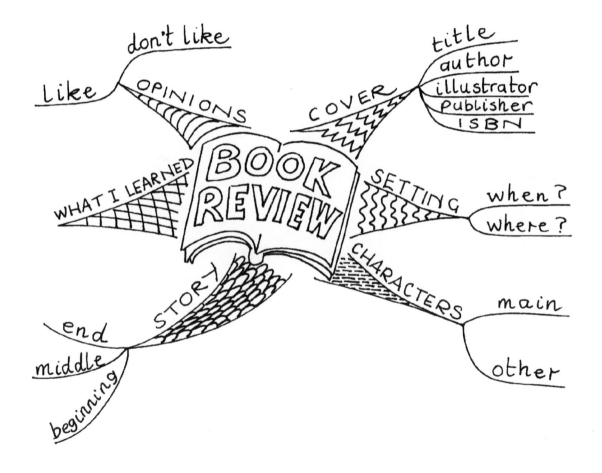

don't like

Like

OPINIONS

title
author
illustrator
publisher
ISBN

COVER

BOOK REVIEW

WHAT I LEARNED

SETTING

when?
where?

STORY

CHARACTERS

main

other

end

middle

beginning

23

Write the book review using your completed map as a plan.

PREPARING AN ORAL PRESENTATION

This activity may be used for motivating children to **find or review information** about any country in the world.
It may also be used to prepare notes for an oral presentation.

Talk with children about one particular country and complete the mind map® with them.

Then ask them to think about any country they would like to know something about
and using books or the internet find the required information to put on the added branches.

When the map is ready,
ask children to write all the information they have collected in a linear format.

Ask the children to remind you of the rules.

- IN THE MIDDLE OF A LANDSCAPE PAGE DRAW A PICTURE REPRESENTING THE TOPIC
- BRANCHES START AT '1 O'CLOCK' AND GO CLOCKWISE AROUND THE PICTURE
- PRINT YOUR WORDS - WRITE ONE WORD ON EACH BRANCH - MAKE THE WORDS 'SIT' ON THE BRANCHES
- DRAW AS MANY PICTURES AS YOU CAN
- USE COLOURS - COLOUR EACH SET OF BRANCHES DIFFERENTLY

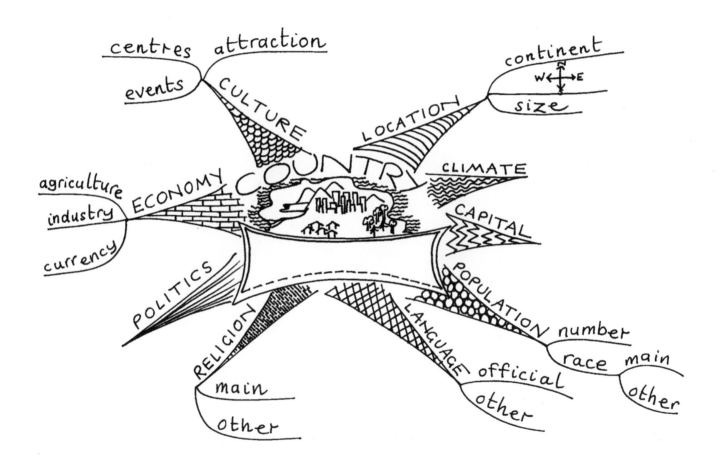

centres   attraction

events   CULTURE

CONTINENT

W ← → E

LOCATION   size

agriculture   ECONOMY   COUNTRY   CLIMATE

industry

CAPITAL

currency

POLITICS   POPULATION   number

RELIGION   LANGUAGE   official   race   main

main   other   other

other

Use the notes on your map and tell someone else everything you have learned about this country.

24

THREE IN ONE
- **CORE BIG PICTURE (AN OVERVIEW)**
- **A REVIEW TOOL**
- **AN ASSESSMENT TOOL**

I   Before you start introducing children to a new topic, it is advisable to give them the BIG PICTURE of what they are going to learn.

       In the centre of a very large sheet of paper, draw a picture representing the topic,
and on thick branches print in big letters the subtopics you are planning to cover.
Share this with the children, explaining a little of what each subtopic will be about.
Mount the map on the wall and, as you teach new things, add thinner branches
and print on them key words giving important information about things children will have to remember
(see examples of developed maps in Activities 29 and 30).

II   You will end up with an excellent, INSTANT, always accessible <u>re**VISION**</u> tool.

       Before you move on to a new subtopic, you can go through the already developed branches.
Later, whenever necessary, you can easily refer to previously covered subtopics.

III   You may give a basic Star Map to children when you want to assess their progress.

       Ask them to expand it by drawing as many thin branches as they need and to put on them key words of the information they have learned about each subtopic.

On the following pages you will find several examples of basic maps which you can use either as activities or for your own reference.
The use of colour cannot be emphasised enough. See, if it makes any difference to you.

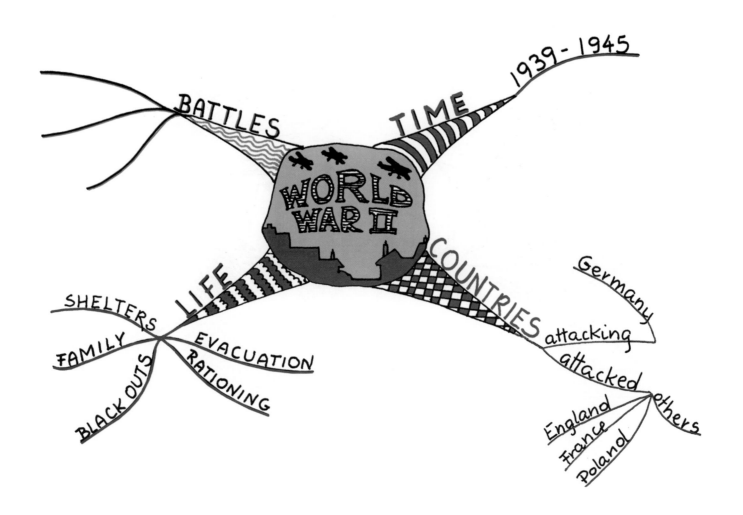

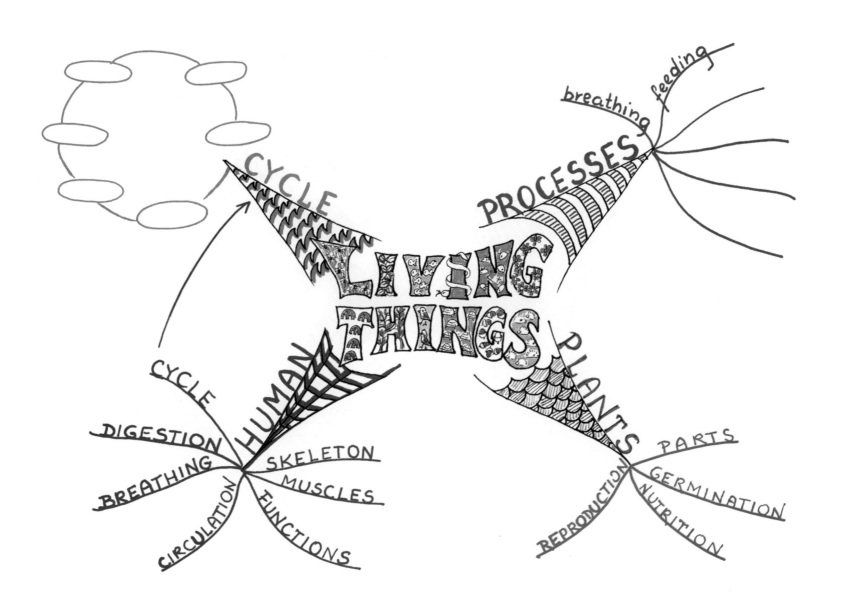

LIVING THINGS

CYCLE

PROCESSES
breathing
feeding

PLANTS
PARTS
GERMINATION
NUTRITION
REPRODUCTION

HUMAN
CYCLE
DIGESTION
BREATHING
CIRCULATION
SKELETON
MUSCLES
FUNCTIONS

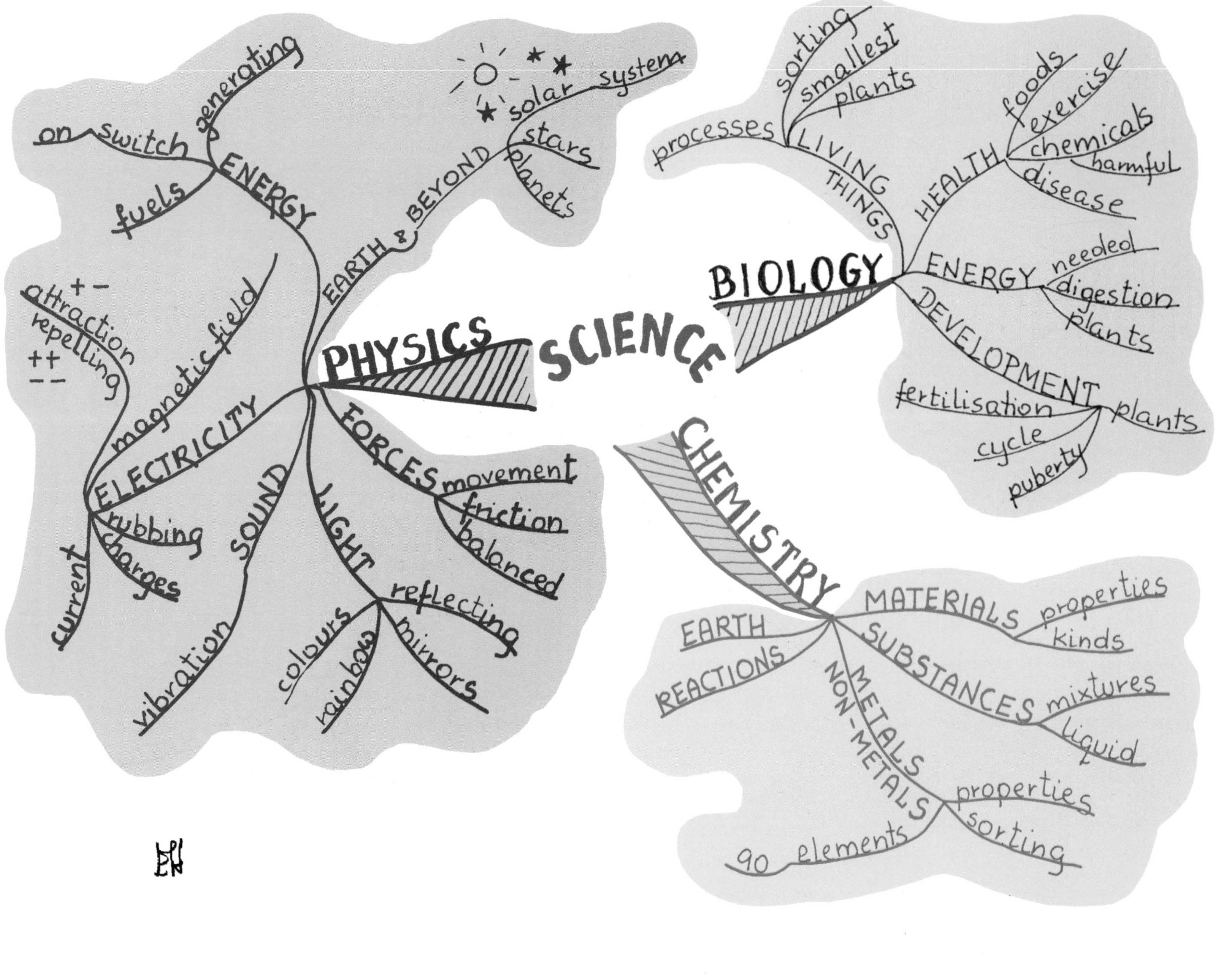
SCIENCE
PHYSICS
ENERGY
on
switch
generating
fuels
EARTH & BEYOND
solar system
stars
planets
ELECTRICITY
+ −
attraction
repelling
++
− −
magnetic field
rubbing
charges
current
SOUND
vibration
LIGHT
reflecting
mirrors
colours
rainbow
FORCES
movement
friction
balanced
BIOLOGY
LIVING THINGS
processes
sorting
smallest
plants
HEALTH
foods
exercise
chemicals
harmful
disease
ENERGY
needed
digestion
plants
DEVELOPMENT
fertilisation
plants
cycle
puberty
CHEMISTRY
MATERIALS
properties
kinds
EARTH
REACTIONS
SUBSTANCES
mixtures
liquid
METALS
NON-METALS
properties
sorting
90 elements

REVISING

Mind mapping a textbook or a revision book is a very useful and effective revision technique.

Following these simple steps will lead you to the 'Grand Map':

- – read the table of contents, highlight key words in every heading and subtitle
    (if the book does not belong to you, make a copy of the contents pages so you can mark them),
  – look at the words you have marked and put them in 'subtopic groups', find a common key word for each group,
  – count the number of main subtopics, this will indicate the number of thick branches and help you plan
    the position of branches on the page;
- draw a colour picture representing your topic or write the textbook/revision book title in the centre of a large sheet of
    paper (A3 or larger, if possible) and draw the main branches;
- now browse through the chapters one by one, highlighting key words in headings and subtitles, words written in bold
    type and any other words that stand out;
- draw thin branches coming out of the main thick branches, add details and any information you consider important,
    PRINTING WORDS and making the letters **big** so that they are easily visible from a distance
    (some children stick their revision maps to the ceiling above their beds).

> Remember the Mind Mapping Rules? Illustrate concepts with as many pictures,
graphs and symbols as you can. Ideally draw every branch in a different colour;

> Every day before your exam put the key words into full sentences - talk somebody
'*around*' your grand map (speak aloud, so you can also hear it);
talk to a friend, your parents or even your pet (!).

Now you are ready to show your friend how to mindmap a revision book.

REVISING

Teaching children to make Subject Revision maps is one of the best things you can do for them as learners.
When they see how useful the tool is, many will still use it to study for their GCSEs and A-levels
as well as for their college exams!
Many of my (Eva's) former students tell me that mind mapping has stayed with them
and that they use it extensively in their professional lives.

Subject revision maps are particularly useful for Year 6 SATS work.

Here is what we need to do (by now we have done all the work in preparation for this 'final' exercise):

- draw a picture of the subject in the middle of a large sheet
- draw as many thick branches as many subtopics we have covered (colouring each in a different colour)
- draw thin branches coming out of the thick ones; print on them key words to represent the information you want to remember
- draw as many pictures as possible, they help us to remember things.

If, for whatever reason, you need to make a one-colour mind map®, you can still either separate each branch family with a colour line or put them in 'colour clouds', as shown in the examples. It is easily done with the use of highlighters, but be warned
- some manufacturers use solvents which can virtually dissolve your beautiful notes.
Colouring pencils are much safer.

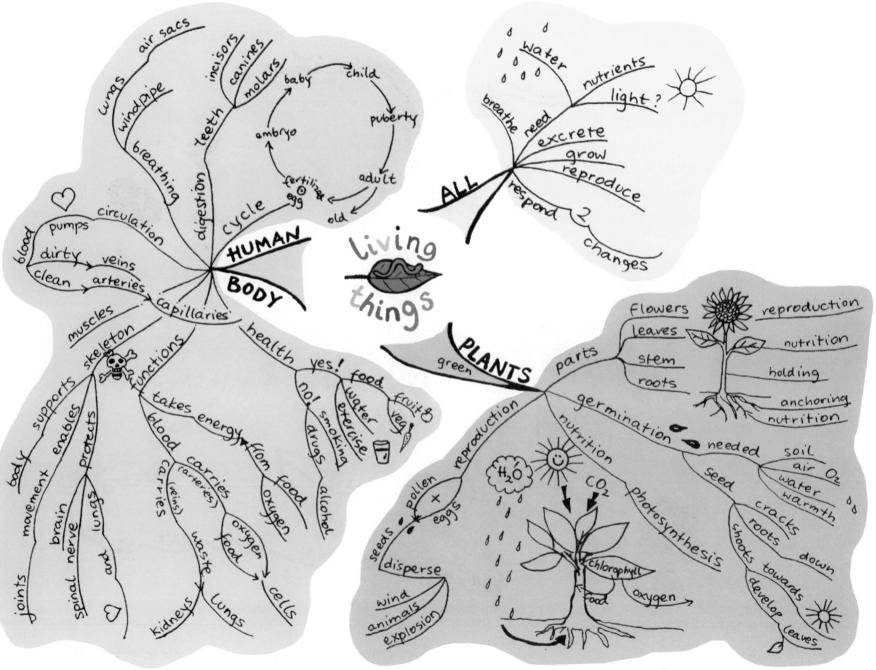

living things

HUMAN BODY

lungs · air sacs
windpipe
breathing
teeth · incisors · canines · molars
digestion
cycle · embryo · fertilized egg · baby · child · puberty · adult · old
circulation · pumps
blood · dirty · veins
clean · arteries
capillaries
muscles
skeleton
functions · supports · body
enables · movement
protects · brain and lungs · nerve · spinal · joints
takes energy · from food
blood carries (arteries) · oxygen · food · cells
carries (veins) · waste · kidneys · Lungs
health · yes! · food · fruit · veg · water · exercise
no! · smoking · drugs · alcohol

ALL
need · water · nutrients · light ?
breathe · excrete · grow · reproduce · respond · 2 changes

PLANTS
green
parts · Flowers · leaves · stem · roots · reproduction · nutrition · holding · anchoring · nutrition
reproduction · pollen + eggs · seeds · disperse · wind · animals · explosion
germination · needed · soil · air O2 · water · warmth · cracks · roots · down · shoots towards · develop leaves · seed
nutrition · photosynthesis · H2O · CO2 · chlorophyll · food · oxygen

©Justina Langley

© Nikki Langley (11 years old)

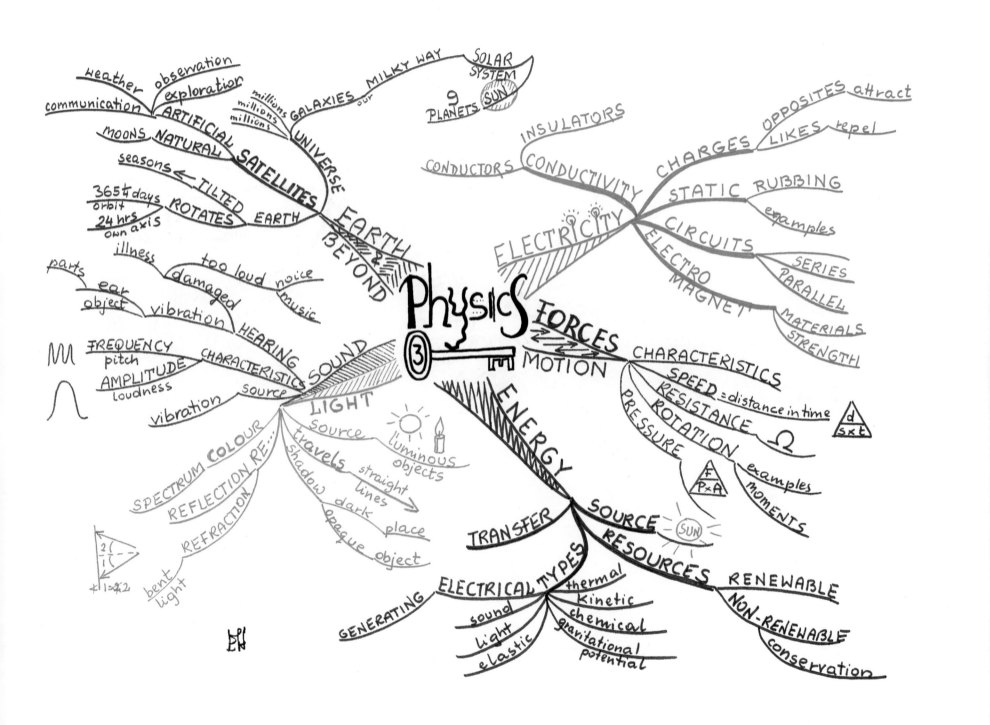

Physics ③

EARTH & BEYOND

- **ARTIFICIAL SATELLITES**
  - communication
  - weather
  - observation
  - exploration
- **NATURAL SATELLITES**
  - MOONS
- **UNIVERSE**
  - GALAXIES — MILKY WAY (our)
  - millions millions millions
  - SOLAR SYSTEM — SUN
  - 9 PLANETS
- **EARTH**
  - TILTED → seasons
  - ROTATES
    - orbit — 365¼ days
    - own axis — 24 hrs

SOUND

- **HEARING**
  - ear — parts
  - object
  - illness
  - damaged
  - too loud
  - noise
  - music
  - vibration
- **CHARACTERISTICS**
  - FREQUENCY — pitch
  - AMPLITUDE — loudness
  - source
  - vibration

LIGHT

- **COLOUR** — SPECTRUM
- **REFLECTION RE...**
- **REFRACTION** — bent light
  - 1 = 2 / 1 = 2
- source
  - LUMINOUS objects
- travels — straight lines
- shadow
  - dark place
  - opaque object

ELECTRICITY

- **CONDUCTIVITY**
  - INSULATORS
  - CONDUCTORS
- **CHARGES**
  - OPPOSITES attract
  - LIKES repel
- **STATIC** — RUBBING
  - examples
- **CIRCUITS**
  - SERIES
  - PARALLEL
- **ELECTRO MAGNET**
  - MATERIALS
  - STRENGTH

FORCES

- **CHARACTERISTICS**
  - SPEED = distance in time
  - RESISTANCE — Ω
  - PRESSURE
  - ROTATION
    - examples
    - moments
  - $\frac{F}{P \times A}$
  - $\frac{d}{s \times t}$
- **MOTION**

ENERGY

- **TRANSFER**
- **SOURCE** — SUN
- **RESOURCES**
  - RENEWABLE
  - NON-RENEWABLE
  - conservation
- **ELECTRICAL** — GENERATING
- **TYPES**
  - thermal
  - kinetic
  - chemical
  - gravitational
  - potential
  - sound
  - light
  - elastic

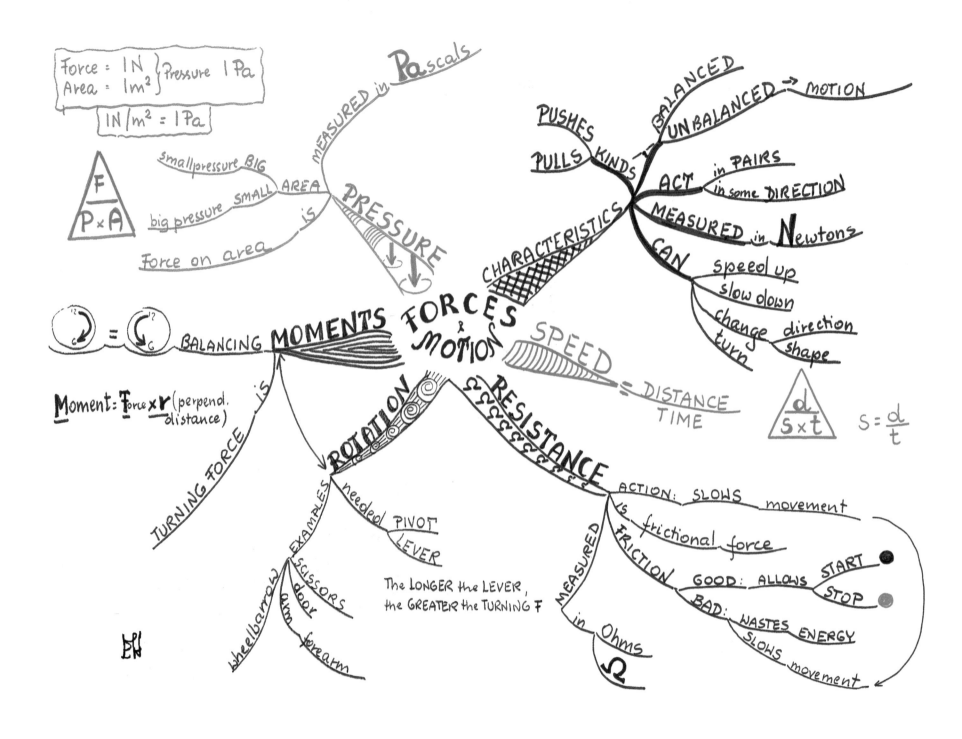

FORCES & MOTION

PRESSURE

Force = 1N
Area = 1m² } Pressure 1 Pa

1N/m² = 1 Pa

$\dfrac{F}{P \times A}$

small pressure BIG

big pressure SMALL **AREA**

Force on area   is

MEASURED in **Pa**scals

CHARACTERISTICS

PUSHES

PULLS KINDS → BALANCED

UNBALANCED → MOTION

ACT   in PAIRS

in some DIRECTION

MEASURED in **Newtons**

CAN

speed up
slow down
change   direction
turn   shape

SPEED

= DISTANCE / TIME

$\dfrac{d}{S \times t}$ $S = \dfrac{d}{t}$

MOMENTS

BALANCING

Moment: **F**orce **× r** (perpend. distance)

TURNING FORCE   is

ROTATION

EXAMPLES

needed PIVOT
LEVER

wheelbarrow
scissors
door
arm
forearm

The LONGER the LEVER, the GREATER the TURNING **F**

RESISTANCE

ACTION: SLOWS movement

is frictional force

FRICTION   GOOD: ALLOWS START
                        STOP

BAD: WASTES ENERGY
     SLOWS movement

MEASURED in Ohms
              Ω

An additional activity: MIND MAPPING FOR YOU!

You may one day decide that planning your work using mind mapping is much more fun than doing it in a linear format.

Here is an example of how Yvonne has planned Tom's Individual Learning Programme.
Tom had no difficulties understanding his targets and achievements,
he read the map with ease, and loved it!

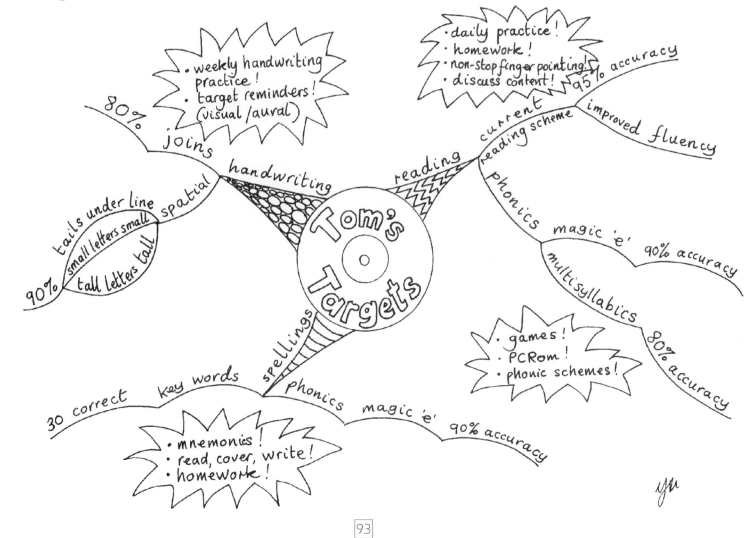

RECOMMENDED MIND MAPPING BIBLIOGRAPHY

Tony Buzan, *How to Mind Map*. Harper Collins 2002, ISBN 0007153732

Tony Buzan with Barry Buzan, *The Mind Map® Book*. BBC Books 2003, ISBN 0563487011

Tony Buzan, *Mind Maps for Kids*. Harper Collins 2003, ISBN 0007151330

Eva Hoffman, *Introducing Children to Mind Mapping in 12 Easy Steps*. Learn To Learn 2001, ISBN 0953538745

Eva Hoffman and Zdzislaw Bartkowicz, *The Learning Adventure*. Learn To Learn 1999, ISBN 0953538702

Lana Israel and Tony Buzan, *Learning with Lana*. The Buzan Centres 1995

Nancy Margulies, *Mapping Inner Space*. Zephyr Press 2001, ISBN 1569761388

Vanda North and Tony Buzan, *Get Ahead*. The Buzan Centres 1991, ISBN 1874374007

OTHER RECOMMENDED TITLES

Edward de Bono, *Lateral Thinking: A Texbook of Creativity*. Penguin Books 1990, ISBN 0140137793

Edward de Bono, *Teach Your Child How to Think*. Viking 1992, ISBN 0670830135

Edward de Bono, *De Bono's Thinking Course*. BBC Books 1994, ISBN 0562270734

Tony Buzan, *Brain Child*. Harper Collins 2003, ISBN 0007166079

Eva Hoffman, *Introducing Children to Their Intelligences*. Learn To Learn 2001, ISBN 0953538729

Eva Hoffman, *Introducing Children to Their Senses*. Learn To Learn 2001, ISBN 0953538737

Eva Hoffman, *Introducing Children to Their Amazing Brains*. Learn To Learn 2001, ISBN 0953538753

Eva Hoffman and Susan Norman, *Stepping Stones*. Saffire Press 2004, ISBN 1901564096

Susan Norman, *Transforming Learning*. Saffire Press (on behalf of SEAL) 2003, ISBN 1901564061

Eva Hoffman: -
'Yvonne's enthusiasm for mind mapping is contagious and the creative ways of using mind mapping with children she teaches truly inspirational, as is her determination to spread the word among her colleagues and friends.'

A teacher, teacher-educator, university lecturer and author of a number of books, Eva has been passionate about understanding the ways in which people learn for longer than she wishes to remember.

Originally trained as an art teacher, Yvonne teaches SEN children and is now focusing on children with dyslexia. At present she is the SEN co-ordinator in Custom House Lane C. P. School in Connah's Quay, a school where innovation is not only welcomed, but positively encouraged.

'Eva has inspired me to use accelerated learning techniques in all my lessons. I am particularly keen on mind mapping, which truly works wonders with children' - Yvonne Handford

Our thanks go to

Tony Buzan for inventing mind mapping and giving to the world this wonderful and most versatile learning and teaching tool;

Brian Wynne , Kate Fox-Parry and Iona Walker, among many others, for their enthusiastic support, encouragement and determination to help children learn;

Susan Norman for reading the manuscript and making valuable comments and suggestions;

Justina and Nikki Langley for letting us include their maps in our book;

all the children who happily and enthusiastically helped us in our research by trying out different activities.